To Ibrahim, Sinan, Erol, and Semih. Love always. —M.O.Y.
For Ammi, Baba, Apa, and Bhai. —M.Q.

•◆•

"If anyone travels on a road in search of knowledge,
God will cause him to travel on one of the roads of Paradise. The angels
will lower their wings in their great pleasure with one who seeks knowledge.
The inhabitants of the heavens and the Earth and (even) the fish in the deep
waters will ask forgiveness for the learned man. The superiority of the learned
over the devout is like that of the moon, on the night when it is full, over the
rest of the stars. The learned are the heirs of the Prophets, and the Prophets do
not leave behind gold or silver coins but rather they leave behind knowledge."
(Hadith 3641)

One Wish: Fatima al-Fihri and the World's Oldest University
Text copyright © 2022 by M. O. Yuksel
Illustrations copyright © 2022 by Mariam Quraishi
All rights reserved. Manufactured in the United States of America.
No part of this book may be used or reproduced in any manner whatsoever without written permission except in the case of
brief quotations embodied in critical articles and reviews. For information address HarperCollins Children's Books,
a division of HarperCollins Publishers, 195 Broadway, New York, NY 10007.
www.harpercollinschildrens.com

ISBN 978-0-06-303291-0

The artist used gouache and watercolor on Arches hot pressed paper to create the illustrations for this book.
Hand lettering by Leah Palmer Preiss
22 23 24 25 PC 10 9 8 7 6 5 4 3 2 1
❖
First Edition

ONE WISH

Fatima al-Fihri and the World's Oldest University

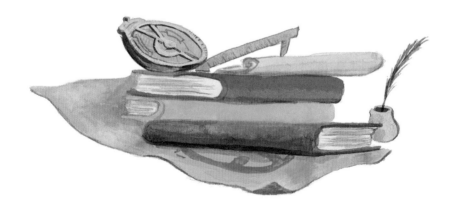

Written by **M. O. Yuksel**   *Illustrated by* **Mariam Quraishi**

HARPER

An Imprint of HarperCollinsPublishers

Fatima craved knowledge like desert flowers crave rain.
Iqra—"read"—was the first word she recited from the Qur'an,
inspiring her love of learning. Unknown worlds opened to her
like a window as she read.
Fatima's heart swelled with excitement—
she wanted to know
how birds flew,
why the sky was blue,
and how flowers grew.
Her passion for learning pulsed through her veins.
She had one wish.
And this wish grew inside her.

In the early ninth century, when Fatima
was a child, boys went to school, and girls
like Fatima were tutored at home.
Fatima's cozy home hummed like a
harmonious melody:
The pages of the Qur'an rustled as Fatima
recited the chapters.
Her quill pen scribbled on her study board
as she solved her math lessons.
Fatima's finger glided on paper as she
traced her favorite lines of literature . . .

while the soothing call to prayer from the
tall minarets of mosques filled the air.

Fatima's faith taught her that knowledge was like
the full moon—lighting the dark night bright.
Her one wish grew stronger.

Here was her wish: to build a school for all. Fatima imagined her school—the chatter of students, stacks of books, geometric patterns, and calligraphic designs. She could almost touch each brick and stone.

But *how* could she bring her one wish to life?
She didn't know how yet, but she believed she could.
She stood tall, determined, and strong,
carrying her wish inside her.

Fatima continued to study hard.
Until one day . . .

Her peaceful life turned into smoke and flames.
War erupted in her town. Fatima and her family
had to flee the only home she'd ever known.

They escaped to the big, bustling city of Fez, Morocco,
to start a new life.
Fatima's heart ached.
Would she find a new home?
Would she continue her education?
Would she fit in?
Fatima tried with all her heart not to crumble.
She stood tall, determined, and strong,
cradling her wish inside her.

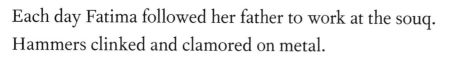

Each day Fatima followed her father to work at the souq.
Hammers clinked and clamored on metal.
Donkeys brayed carrying overflowing baskets on their backs.
Moroccan mint tea splashed noisily from silver pots . . .
while the soothing call to prayer from the tall minarets of
mosques filled the air.
The souq eased her worries and made her feel at home.

As Fatima grew older, one sound rose above the others—the lively debates about the stars, planets, and distant lands and languages captivated her.

Oh, how Fatima wished for a school where these scholars could teach all students.

Fatima imagined her school—feet shuffling from class to class, scholars lecturing at every corner of the building, students debating in various dialects. . . . She could almost touch each brick and stone. But *how* could she bring her wish to life?

She still didn't know how yet, but she believed she could.
She stood tall, determined, and strong,
nurturing her wish inside her.

Days turned into years as Fatima became a young lady and got married.

Through hard work and persistence, Fatima and her family became wealthy merchants.

But their good fortune didn't last—her husband
and father died of an illness.

Fatima, alone and grieving, had to decide what to do next.

Fatima's faith taught her that charity— sadaqah jariyah—was like planting a single seed from which thousands of wildflowers continuously bloomed. She wondered how she could use the fortune left to her by her father and husband to honor them and to serve the community she so loved.

As she watched more people arrive daily in Fez, she knew what to do. Fez had opened its arms to her, and she wanted to do the same for those in need.

Fatima's wish burned brightly inside her.

Fatima knew the best way to help her community was to build a school where students, especially the poor and the refugees, could live and study for free.

Her wish was a school where scholars from around the world could teach about history, geometry, poetry, and more. A school where students could earn degrees and become anything they wanted—doctors, teachers, and scientists. Fatima knew she could finally build her school. She purchased the land and started planning.

As the first stone was laid, Fatima promised to fast each day from dawn to dusk until the work was complete. The days were long and hot, but Fatima did not eat or drink until the sun set. Her throat burned from thirst, and her stomach grumbled with hunger. But Fatima's wish fueled her. Fasting was her way of showing her passion, gratitude, and faith.

She stood tall, determined, and strong.
Her devotion ran deep.

Fatima oversaw each detail of the school—the intricate mosaics on the walls, ceramic patterns on the floors, wooden carvings on the ceilings, even the type of stone to use. She made every decision.

Fatima knew her school was like planting a single seed that would continuously bloom with each student who studied there. Her school, which was also a mosque and a library, opened its arms ready to serve the community Fatima so loved. It was named the al-Qarawiyyin, after her hometown in Tunisia.

After two long years, the final brick was laid.
Fatima's heart burst with joy!
She prayed in gratitude in her mosque.

Soon the school echoed with the harmonious melody of feet shuffling
from class to class,
scholars lecturing at every corner of the building,
students from all over the world debating in various dialects . . .
while the soothing call to prayer from the tall minarets of mosques filled the air.
Her wish had come true!

Fatima's heart soared with pride.
Her wish—*her* school—stood tall, determined, and strong.
Just like her.
Fatima's passion for learning pulsed
through the school,
through her community,
and throughout the world.

Her school guided scholars for thousands of years.

And it still thrives.

Like many people, I was unaware of Fatima al-Fihri until I attended the exhibit *1001 Inventions* in New York City in 2010. I was surprised and enamored by this visionary, trailblazing woman who founded the oldest existing and continually operating university in the world. I had to share her story!

Fatima al-Fihri, also written as Fatima al-Fihriya, was born in approximately 800 CE in Tunisia. Little is known about her childhood or private life; hence, I took the liberty of reconstructing her early years based on historical and cultural information. However, we do know that she was the daughter of a wealthy businessman, scholar, and jurist, Mohammad al-Fihri, who valued education very much. Fatima and her sister, Mariam, were well educated and devoutly pious. Both sisters were well versed in religion, the hadith, and other subjects such as math and literature.

We also know that Fatima and her family migrated to Fez, Morocco, which was a thriving metropolis and a stable oasis especially for refugees fleeing unstable regions. She and her sister, Mariam, inherited a fortune from their father after he died from an illness. Fatima also inherited money from her husband. The sisters decided to invest their money to benefit their community in the form of a sadaqah jariyah—continuous charity. Mariam built the Andalusian Mosque in Fez, now considered one of the oldest mosques in the world. Fatima built the al-Qarawiyyin Mosque, considered one of the oldest existing institutions of higher education in the world. From the very beginning, Fatima's mosque distinguished itself from others because of its focus on education. The king of Morocco, Yahya I, and the scholarly community of Fez supported Fatima's vision of an institution of higher education. The al-Qarawiyyin functioned as a school from its inception, and it welcomed both men and women. According to historians, female scholars such as Alia Bint-Tayeb Benkirane also taught at al-Qarawiyyin.

Mosques, also called masjid, served as the first institutions of higher education beginning in the seventh century. Besides being a house of worship and providing spaces for social gatherings, a mosque also functioned as an educational institution that taught religious and secular topics such as math, science, history, law, and literature. According to historians, the original structure Fatima al-Fihri built also had a library, which later burned down in a fire and was refurbished. Al-Qarawiyyin was substantially expanded by future generations of rulers and was a famous center of learning that attracted scholars from around the globe.

Fatima al-Fihri played an important role in the advancement of education and civilization. She is admired by many for her perseverance, wisdom, and generosity. Almost 1,200 years have passed, and al-Qarawiyyin University continues to share the gift of knowledge. Fatima is an inspiration to all, and her rich legacy lives on in the excellence of the institution she founded.

THE UNIVERSITY OF AL-QARAWIYYIN

The University of al-Qarawiyyin (also spelled al-Karaouine, al-Quaraouiyine, al-Karawiyyīn) was established in 859 CE in Fez, Morocco, by Fatima al-Fihri. It is the oldest existing and continually operating educational institution in the world according to UNESCO and Guinness World Records. Other historical sites may date back further, but al-Qarawiyyin holds the record for continuously offering education since its founding.

The University of al-Qarawiyyin has served as a key center of cultural and religious exchange and academic relations between the Islamic world and Europe for centuries. Historians have argued that the first Western universities like the University of Bologna, Oxford, Cambridge, and Harvard were modeled after Islamic institutions of higher education, especially regarding endowments, scholarships, chairs of departments, and dormitories.

It is claimed that some of the University of al-Qarawiyyin's famous alumni include the first French pope, Pope Sylvester II, who introduced Arabic numerals and the use of zero to Europe; the philosopher and physician Maimonides, who wrote the first books on Jewish law; the geographer al-Idrisi, who created the most accurate map of the world at the time; and the philosopher Ibn Rushd, also known as Averroes, who wrote many famous books about medicine, physics, and philosophy.

The university is still in operation today and continues to grant degrees in various religious and physical sciences.

GLOSSARY

Fast: To abstain from food and drink from dawn to dusk.

Hadith: Sayings and customs of Prophet Muhammad and his companions.

Inheritance: To receive something such as property and money from someone after their death.

Iqra: Arabic word which means to read or recite.

Islam: Complete voluntary submission to God.

Minaret: A tall, slender tower; part of a mosque.

Mosque: Place of worship for Muslims. Also referred to as a masjid, jamii, or Islamic center.

Muslim: People who practice the religion of Islam.

Prophet: Someone who delivers a message from God to people.

Quill pen: A writing tool made from a bird feather.

Qur'an: Holy book of Islam. It is also spelled as Quran or Koran.

Refugee: A person forced to leave their country to escape war or natural disaster.

Sadaqah jariyah: Continuous, ongoing voluntary charity.

Souq: Marketplace.

University: Degree-granting institution of higher learning, with undergraduate and graduate programs.

ACKNOWLEDGMENTS

My sincere and eternal gratitude to Dr. Matthew Schumann of Princeton University for his invaluable input and guidance throughout the preparation of this book. Also, many thanks to Dr. Fatima Siddiqi of Fez University, Dr. Abdullah Yildirim of Istanbul University, the Highlights Foundation, Kate Messner, and Sarah Albee for their generous guidance and support.

BIBLIOGRAPHY

Abun-Nasr, Jamil M., ed. *A History of the Maghrib in the Islamic Period*. Cambridge University Press, 1987.

Akyeampong, Emmanuel K., and Henry Louis Gates, Jr., eds. *Dictionary of African Biography*. Oxford University Press, 2012.

Al-Kattani, Yusuf. *Madrasat al-Imam al-Bukhari fi al-Maghrib*. Dar Lisan al-`Arab, 1980.

Al-Tazi, 'Abd al-Hadi, *Jami 'al-Qarawiyyin*. 2nd Ed. Rabat, Morocco: 2000.

Dossett, Rena D. "The historical influence of classical Islam on western humanistic education." *International Journal of Social Science and Humanity 4*, no. 2 (2014): 88.

Gunther, Sebastian. "Education, general (up to 1500)," in *Encyclopedia of Islam Three*. Kate Fleet, Gudrun Kramer, Denis Matringe, John Nawas, Everett Rowson, eds. Brill, 2017.

Joseph, Suad, and Afsaneh Najmabadi. *Encyclopedia of Women & Islamic Cultures: Economics, Education, Mobility and Space*. Brill, 2003.

Kenny, Jeffrey T., and Ebrahim Moosa. *Islam in the Modern World*. Routledge, 2014.

Landau, Rom. *Morocco: Marrakesh, Fez, Rabat*. Putnam, 1967.

Lulat, Y. G. M. *A History of African Higher Education from Antiquity to the Present: A Critical Synthesis Studies in Higher Education*. Greenwood Publishing Group, 2005.

Makdisi, George. *The Rise of Colleges: Institutions of Learning in Islam and the West*. Edinburgh University Press, 1981.

Nakosteen, Mehdi. *History of Islamic Origins of Western Education A.D. 800–1350*. University of Colorado Press, 1964.

Souad, Merah, Tahraoui Ramdane, and Mariya Senim Khan. "Fatimah Al-Fihri and Religious Fraternity in Al-Qarawiyyin University: A Case Study." *International Journal of Humanities and Social Science*, vol. 7, no. 10, 2017, pp. 177-183.

Swartley, Keith E. *Encountering the World of Islam*. InterVarsity Press, 2005.

Websites:

www.muslimheritage.com/article/al-qarawiyyin-mosque-and-university

www.morocco.com/blog/the-al-qarawiyyin-mosque

www.dw.com/en/fatima-al-fihri-founder-of-the-worlds-oldest-university/a-53371150

For Kids:

www.kids.nationalgeographic.com/explore/countries/morocco/#morrocco-marrakech-market.jpg

www.ducksters.com/geography/country.php?country=Morocco

www.childrensuniversity.manchester.ac.uk/learning-activities/student-life/an-introduction-to-student-life/the-benefits-of-a-higher-education/

TIMELINE

of al-Qarawiyyin and some of the famous scholars associated with the university

859 • Fatima al-Fihri builds al-Qarawiyyin.

946–1003 • Scientist Gerbert d'Aurillac, who later became Pope Sylvester II, studies at al-Qarawiyyin and introduces the Arabic numeral system and the concept of zero to Europe.

956 • al-Qarawiyyin is expanded by the Ummayyed Dynasty.

1038 • Famous scholars Abu Imran al-Fassi and Abu Ali al-Kali teach Malekite jurisprudence and literature, respectively, at al-Qarawiyyin.

1076–1148 • Judge and scholar of Maliki law Abu Bakr Ibn al-Arabi writes books about history and religion.

1085–1138 • Abu Bakr Muhammad Ibn Yahya, also known as Avempace, writes about philosophy, medicine, astronomy, and physics. He was also a musician and poet.

1100–1165 • Muhammad al-Idrisi creates the most accurate map of the world at the time.

1126–1198 • Ibn Rushd, also known as Averroes, writes many famous books about medicine, physics, and philosophy.

1135–1143 • al-Qarawiyyin is expanded by the Almoravid Dynasty.

1135–1204 • Jewish philosopher and theologian Moses ben Maimon, also known as Maimonides, writes the first books on Jewish law.

1165–1240 • Ibn al-Arabi writes books on Islamic mysticism and philosophy.

1204 • Nur al-Din al-Bitruji, also known as Alpetragius, writes about astronomy and philosophy.

1302 • Ibn Ajroum writes a grammar book.

1313–1374 • Lisan al-Dine Ibn al-Khatib writes books about history.

1332–1406 • Ibn Khaldun writes books on and is a pioneer of historiography, sociology, economics, and demography.

1359 • The Marinid dynasty expands the al-Qarawiyyin library.

1494–1554 • Geographer and diplomat Hassan al-Wazzan, also known as Leo Africanus, writes the influential book *Description of Africa*.

1495–1542 • Nicolas Clenard, professor at Louvain University in Belgium, exports to Europe the University of al-Qarawiyyin's intellectual and scientific work, like Ibn Baklarech's medical treatise.

1596–1667 • Jacob Golius translates Arabic texts such as the astronomical treatise of Al-Farghani and writes an Arabic-Latin dictionary.

1947 • al-Qarawiyyin integrates into the Moroccan state education system.

1963 • al-Qarawiyyin becomes part of the Moroccan state university system.

AL-QARAWIYYIN COURTYARD, 2021